CW00493843

THE REAL ESTATE INVESTOR FOR BEGINNERS

How to Finance and Invest with No Money Down Up to Be A Millionaire in the Realtor Business. Residential and Commercial Market

Contents

Introduction

What is the Real Estate Market: Understand about this popular investment? What is real estate is an issue that has been widely discussed over the years? Regarding this respect, those who express the demand for what the real estate market is are investors in real estate and durable goods. In addition to the real estate funds industry, which is a very active vertical. Based on this context, we can define what the real estate market is: it is nothing more than a trade in the real estate sector that negotiates land or any occupation built in a given space. Generally, those active in the market are, among others, individuals, legal entities, and real estate agents, who act as intermediaries for the sale or rental of properties, such as houses and apartments, rooms, and offices. With the economy rebuilding, the real estate market in 2019 has a strong prominence in its growth. With low inflation, the consumer gains purchasing power. Greater consumer confidence - The resumption of the economy makes investors feel confident again.

Modernization of home automation - In order to attract buyers, construction companies have invested in technology and other differentials. Use of virtual reality - Have you ever imagined being able to visit an enterprise that has not yet been built? Creation of more real estate platforms - More attractive ads, features, and data optimization in the real estate market, is it better to buy land or property? Real estate market there are advantages and disadvantages, so it is necessary to be well informed about the possibilities. It is important to take into account the amount available for the investment and the desired time. One of the main advantages of buying land and building a house is the idealization of the property.

However, designing a home the way you want it takes time and skilled labor. However, a finished house is something that may be more practical, but it may be necessary to make some modifications. Know some risks that can plague the real estate market. In fact, it is necessary to pay attention to some risks in the real estate market.

Market Risk - It represents fluctuations in the price of the property, in addition to the fluctuation in other variables involved in the transaction.

Liquidity Risk - It may be that the moment you want to recover your investment in the market, there are simply no interested buyers.

Credit risk - In this case, if a buyer has problems honoring the property payment, the return may be compromised.

Accident risk - Accidents caused by human failures such as fires or simple poorly planned engineering.

Expropriation risk - If the government decides to expropriate the location of its land, unfortunately, in this case, there is not much to do.

FIIs are an option for those who want to invest in the real estate market. If the intention is to buy a property to rent or build and sell, Real Estate Investment Funds (FIIs) may be an option. In short, real estate funds are like closed condominiums, where investors come together in order to invest their resources. It is worth mentioning that they are investments with variable income and traded on the stock exchange. Still, applying in FII is an extremely smart way for an investor who wants to invest. Therefore, with much fewer resources than you would need to buy a property, in an FII, you can buy shares and obtain monthly income.

To enter the real estate market, the investor needs to be aware that the return of the application, be it the construction of houses, purchase in the plant, buildings or subdivisions, occurs after the time of the work, and this can mean a delay of 18 to 36 months, depending on the size of the enterprise and availability of labor.

The most basic way to enter the real estate market is to acquire a property, an operation that requires full payment of the asset or most of the entry price, and the remainder in approved credit. It is also possible to invest in fractions of a property, participating in the profit obtained from the sale or rent of the properties, for example. The value is proportional to the number of shares sold, divided among all buyers. Some precautions are essential to ensure that such investments provide a good return. When investing, the client must identify whether the region of interest has potential for growth in infrastructure and expansion, a view of the real estate market potential for the region, supermarkets, schools, hospitals, and accessibility.

Chapter 1: Who Is A Typical Real Estate Investor?

Real estate investment is not a new adventure. While this might be your first-time diving into the topic, you should know that you are about to enter into the league of real men and women. Yes, real estate investment is an industry where real and tough people operates.

Before we go deep into real estate investment, the basics must first be ironed out. And the first of such is understanding who a typical real estate investor is.

If you are tired of living in debt or having to leave from hand to mouth, then you can be sure that real estate is a profitable industry. If you have been doing well for yourself financially but looking to increase your cash flow, you are also welcome to the league of real men and women.

Without mixing words, a typical real estate investor is one who evaluates the real estate market and purchases property with the sole intention of building wealth. Depending on your investment objectives, you can purchase a residential or commercial property or even a combination of both.

Real estate investment is profitable. You can invest in real estate with little or no money and go on to be a millionaire. While there are many ways to go about that, you need to know the steps and have the right skills to aid your journey – all of which you will be taught in later chapters of this book.

However, before that, what is more important is to know and function as a real estate investor. When the excitement of the opportunity to start a new adventure wears off, what will remain is your understanding of who a typical real estate investor is.

One of the first things the real estate investor must understand is the difference between residential and commercial markets and which one he would be interested in investing in.

Residential and Commercial Markets

Residential properties include townhouses, apartments and single-family homes. In simpler terms, residential properties are properties where people live. You as the property owner can decide to live in the property or rent out the entire property and enjoy the rental income. In residential properties, your tenants will most likely be individuals and families.

Commercial property, on the other hand, includes office space, industrial buildings, public facilities, retail shops, hotels ad so much more. As it is evident, one major difference between commercial properties have from residential ones is that while residential properties are leased out to individuals and families, commercial properties are characterized by businesses as tenants.

Just like in the residential property, however, commercial property owners can decide to operate from the property they own and lease the rest of the space out to tenants or lease all of the property out. Commercial property is, without a doubt, a significant investment market.

Difference Between Residential Property and Commercial Property

Real estate investment is of diverse kinds. However, we will be focusing on two of the most popular ones in this book. Here, we look into the differences between residential properties and commercial properties. And the reason for this is simple.

In your journey as a real estate investor, you will be faced, sooner or later, on which of the markets you should invest in. If you ask a real estate investor in the residential market which of the markets to invest in, he or she will tell you why the residential market is the best and he will be right. Likewise, an investor in the commercial market will also let you know how much he has made in the last month and how that is only possible in his area of operation.

All of that can leave you confused, especially as you are just starting out. However, that is not the case with you. You are smart; you got this book. Let us go over the differences between these markets and you will see why they are different.

- **Property Management**: it is not uncommon for property owners in the residential market to deal with a single household or tenant at a time. Without a doubt, the situation is the exact opposite in commercial markets. Owners can be dealing with up to 25 tenants in a single property. And this comes with serious challenges.

  For instance, in commercial markets, owners will need the service of property managers to assist in rent collection, maintenance and comfortable experience of tenants. It is all of these that help owners keep their tenants happy. In the residential markets, however, this is not often the case. Investors or owners manage the property themselves except in cases when they are not real estate experts and require the services of professionals to aid management and get maximum value from their investment.

- **Proper Investigation**: it should come without a surprise to you that any endeavor you embark upon, real estate inclusive, a proper investigation has to be carried out. In real estate investment, investigations that you must carry out include the title, covenants, reports of buildings and markets fundamentals. These investigations are native to both types of markets.

  However, with commercial property, additional investigations are required. Outstanding warranties, building services condition, operational efficiency, and underlying tenant covenants are some of the required investigations.

- **Risk Profile**: commercial properties are characterized by long-term leases and this helps to provide a more stable cash flows than the residential property that has shorter leases. In residential property leases, tenants have the opportunity of breaking the agreement under short notice and this breeds high risk on the part of the investor.

Commercial property, on the other hand, offers more security. The lease structure in residential property is structured in such a way that investors or owners have to take responsibility for routine maintenance and repairs. In commercial property, the opposite is the case. Tenants are responsible for all property management and repairs.

- **Valuation Variations**: there are also differences in valuation between our most popular real estate investment markets. Irrational valuations are often common in residential markets. And the reason is that the prices of properties in the residential markets are determined by comparing other properties of similar features in the area. This is often beyond the capability of the investors and that leaves you in great risks. Properties in the commercial markets, on the hand, have valuations that are determined by the current value of future income streams.

So, in the end, if you ask any successful real estate investor today about the right market to pursue, I can bet that you will barely find someone who will sincerely tell you should go for one and neglect the other. What thing is common practice though; when investors begin out, they try out the less risky market which is the residential market. When they have gained enough experience in the market, they move on to the commercial market. This is not a template as what you should but it has worked for many, maybe it will work for you.

Meanwhile, the answer to that is embedded in this book. Follow along. In other to put you on the right track as you begin your real estate investment journey, you need to find out what your goal is. And that is what will lead us to the next part.

What Is Your Goal?

If you are asked what is your reason for wanting to go into real estate investment, it is certain that your answer will be that you want to make a healthy return on your income or, simpler terms, generate income. Afterall, that is the reason you have picked this book and that is the promise of this book.

You are right! Even the most successful real estate investor, when asked, will tell you that he is interested in making profits. So, what is wrong with that? Absolutely nothing!

The only issue, when that is all about your mindset, making the profit you have in mind is not guaranteed. And that is where goals set in. you have got to have a well-defined goal.

What exactly do you wish to achieve?

How long do you think it will take you?

What are the things you need to achieve this goal?

These and some others are the questions you must answer. And setting a goal helps you visualize your future right from the beginning. Goals can be threatening if handled wrongly and this is the reason why many don't set goals or the majority of those who do, don't meet their targets.

Goal setting, especially in real estate investment is quite important. Whether you plan on owning all the apartments in an area or having a property in one of the most lucrative areas in the country, it is goal setting that will help you reach there in record time.

In other to set goals that you will live by, there are certain ways to go about it. In real estate investment, there are five kinds of ways to set goals that will ensure you are successful. Let's get to it.

1. **Set Specific Goals**

You are not ready to make a move in real estate if you don't have a specific goal in mind. Yes, you are interested in making profits from your investment, but how exactly do you intend to achieve that? You also need to determine if it is a long-term goal or short term.

You have to clearly state every term within the goal and realize every step that needs to be taken in other to achieve your goal. If you intend to have a particular amount as profits at the end of your first year as a real estate investor, then you will begin to look at what actionable steps you need to take in other to realize this goal.

It is also advisable to write down your goal. Studies have shown that people who write down their goals tend to achieve them unlike those who don't write their goals. When writing your specific goals, some of the questions you must answer is what exactly you are trying to achieve, why the goal is important, how achieving or failing to achieve the goal affect your business. You must also recognize the resources you will need to accomplish your goal and the personnel that will help you achieve your goal.

Mind you, this can be overwhelming. So, if you don't have the answers to all your questions at a go, take your time. But, make sure you set specific goals and let them guide you.

2. Measurable Goal

What is the essence of setting goals that you cannot check if you actually achieved what you set out to do over a period of time? The purpose of your goal will first be achieved if it is measurable. It is this kind of goals that help you to remain motivated as the progress of your goal is known and you are encouraged as the finish line approaches.

Since you are able to know the level you are at every point in time, you also have an understanding of what work is left to be done and that pushes to meet your targets. For instance, if you decide to save a particular amount of money by the end of the year, talking about it will not help you. Rather, saving a certain amount each month will do and you are able to know how much is left as each month went by.

3. Attainable Goal

You will not do yourself much good at any point of your real estate investment endeavor if you begin to set unattainable goal. I believe one of the things that cause people to lose interest in setting goals is having unattainable goals. When this happens, they get frustrated and eventually stop setting goals after some time. You see, the problem is not that they cannot achieve a goal, it is that they have set unattainable and unrealistic goals.

Your goals, however, should push beyond your comfort zone and exhaust your resources and practical enough to accomplish. When you have set attainable goals, you will know if you are ready financially to achieve the goal and if you have indeed given yourself enough time to accomplish the goal. You will also know the challenges you will face in other to achieve the goal.

It is in understanding those that you will be able to come up with solutions to the challenges that can arise and ultimately help you overcome and reach your goal.

4. Relevant Goal

Relevance in real estate investment goal setting refers to setting goals that matter to the current state of your business. While long term goals are valid and encouraged, setting a goal that helps your business' bottom line is what is required.

Relevant goals will eradicate the frustration that irrelevant ones bring. They let you have a clear purpose of what you want to do in real estate investment and how long it will take you to achieve that.

5. Time-Bound Goal

Give your goals a deadline! I don't know of any simple way of saying it. Your goals must have a date or time set against it. You want to attend how many networking events in the next 4 months, or you want to attend an industry conference twice per month for the next six months.

Whatever your goal is, putting a time behind it keeps you focused and ultimately successful. And on other to do that, make sure to celebrate every small and big win that comes your way. This will keep you motivated and charged for the future.

We have seen how important goals are and what must be done to achieve them. Whatever your goals are, make sure they are specific, measurable, attainable, relevant and time-bound. That is your blueprint to success.

Common Problems of New Real Estate Investors

New investors like you will run int problems. It is a jungle out there and without the right guide, you will run into problems that will leave you frustrated and unhappy. Well, you don't have to join the league of frustrated investors, below are some of the common problems you will encounter when just starting out and how to overcome them.

a. **The Property**

A few problems rally around the property. Of course, the property is the major reason for discussion in any real estate investment, so it is ideal that there are issues to run into regarding it. And the first of those problems is getting properties.

Experienced and successful investors have their way around getting information about listings but what about you, the newbie? Your friends here are the local wholesalers and to meet them, you have to attend the local investment club meetings.

I know you must be thinking of where to find out. Easy! The answer is the Real Estate Investment Association. All you have to do is search online about the meeting place and time of the area your area and attend their meeting.

Once you are in the group, of course, the next thing to do is to let them know what you can do. if you have experience in construction. You can let them know that and go on to say you want to buy a property. Because you are a new investor, going ahead to say you are looking for properties may not help you as they will have an investor already.

However, once you are able to create a level of urgency that will eradicate many processes that other investors may want to go through before purchasing their property, you can be sure to land your first property right on the spot.

b. The Money

I bet this shouldn't come as a surprise to you. If you want to buy a property, of course, you should have the money to pay for the current owner. Well, if you don't have the money yet, there are a few options you can use to get the property.

One of the commonest is to secure a short-term loan. The issue is this is very tricky and it often has a high interest rate and that can mean you will pay back with a large percentage of your profit. Short-term loans are often not encouraged but it is a possible option to land your first property.

Another means of getting funds is to have a partner. This helps you to share the burden. However, ensure you both have a legal document written and signed that includes details of your commitments. If that does not work for you, you can as well save your own money. While this might be longer than the first two options mentioned, it is the safest.

c. The Work

It is not uncommon to find that newly acquired property needs renovation. And unless the work required is much and needs expertise, you will have to work there yourself.

If the work is much, it is easy to get contractors to work on your property these days. Telling everyone you know that you need a contractor might do it for you. If not, Craigslist or AngelList are online platforms where you can get contractors to work on your newly acquired property.

Here is where you should be careful though; don't work with uninsured and unlicensed contractors. The risk is too much and you don't want to fall into problems at this early stage. Find out how soon a contractor can start work on your property and ensure you are there to monitor the whole process.

To scale through your early days in the real estate investment, these are some of the mistakes you must avoid.

Chapter 2: Why Banks Won't Loan You Money

If it hasn't happened to you before, you must have heard others say banks turn down their loan offer. Then you begin to wonder why. Most times, the only people banks give loans are those who have money already. It is unfair - at least that has been your thought.

Contrary to popular opinion that banks detest new businesses or investors. That is untrue. The only issue is that the many new real estate investors have discouraging situations around them. Meanwhile, most people approach the bank without having a proper understanding of how a bank loan works.

You must know, without a doubt, that banks give loan for profit earning purposes. And to fulfil this task or purpose, they must have some characteristics. Let us go over the characteristics of a bank loan.

1. Parties

This is primary. In other for a bank loan to successfully happen, two parties must be involved. The first is the bank provides the loan and the other party is you – the applicant. When the applicant applies for a loan in the bank, if he is found to be financially viable, the request is granted, if not, it is rejected outrightly.

2. Amount of Loan

The amount of loan a bank gives an applicant may be small, medium or large. There is always a difference between the applied amount and the sanctioned amount on the basis of the capacity and quality of the borrower. Often time, the purpose for which the loan is requested is also considered.

3. Decision

In bank loan request, the bank has the ultimate decision. It decides who to grant his loan application and who to reject. This decision is reached having considered the creditworthiness of the applicant, its own fund and other issues.

4. Mode of Loan

Except in rare cases, loans are given in cash. However, there are cases when the loan is provided in kind such as machinery, raw materials and other inputs. This is determined based on the purpose of the loan and the applicant creditability.

5. Nature of Disbursement

Banks usually disburse the loan in instalment basis. Except on rare cases, especially when the bank is convinced, it may decide to disburse the whole amount of the sanctioned amount at a time.

6. Process

Bank loans are disbursed through the applicant or client's current account. In the case when the client does not have a current account with the bank, he or she is mandated to open one before the loan is disbursed.

7. Security

One thing that banks don't joke with is the security of the loan. Before a bank accepts a loan application, it must have been assured of collateral that can pay back the loan from the applicant or his guarantor. Cases where the amount of the loan is small, the collateral can be removed and the loan is processed on the basis of personal guarantee.

8. Interest Rate

This is not new – banks never sanction a loan without interest! However, the interest rate can vary depending on the types of the loan and track record of the client.

9. Period

The period of a loan sanctioning can be an immediate, short-term, mid-term or long-term basis. Again, the periodicity of the loan is determined by the bank. And it depends on the type of loan being requested, the creditworthiness of the client and the purpose for which the loan is requested.

10. Repayment of loan

Loans are paid on an installment basis, but they can also be repaid on a one-shot arrangement. Banks repayment schedule are prepared based on the possible cash flow stream of the client's projects.

Having gone through these characteristics of bank loans, you must be wondering, why then do banks reject loan applications. Well, the reasons are not far-fetched.

Let us dig deep into why banks turn the deaf ear when a person, especially a new real estate investor like you approach them for a loan. There are so many reasons why banks will turn down your loan requests. Below are some of the most popular ones.

- **Lack of Consistent Cash Flow**

Banks always want to rely on steady revenue system from the investor coming to request for a loan. So, if you don't fall under the radar of investors with a track record of consistent cash flow, there is a high chance that your request will be turned down.

- **Insufficient Collateral**

Banks rely on the opportunity to sell your property or collateral in the event where you are unable to meet the loan agreements. Since you are not likely to have sufficient collateral, then the bank is most likely going to reject your loan request.

- **Abundance of Debt**

If you have a record of debts with various lenders, chances are no one will be willing to lend you more money. And surprisingly, banks are that way too. No bank will give a new investor any money if they are already owing a lot of people or other banks. The problem here is that it is not uncommon to have new investors have multiple sources to borrow from and that is the right turn off for banks.

- **Economic Concerns**

Banks, like any other business, are interested in making a profit. So, don't be offended if it seems they are more interested in the current economic condition than your purpose. If banks feel the current the economic conditions are not favorable, chances are they won't grant your loan request. You can argue that when the economy is bad, it is hard to maintain revenue and keep costs down, but banks aren't interested in that.

- **Insufficient Operating History**

If you don't have a significant and lengthy track record in your business, chances are banks will not grant your loan request. Banks are only interested in giving funds to an investor or business that has sustained a certain amount of success and credibility. So, often time, before they grant loan request, one of the things they ask for is a document showing a solid track record of generating profits over a period of time.

There are several reasons why banks will not lend you money. But when this happens, what are you expected to do? well, there is a few options new real estate investor like you can look to. Some of these other options listed below are called alternative financing.

a. Merchant Cash Advances

It is a program that lends you a particular sum of capital by purchasing an equivalent amount of your future credit/debit card sales. Unlike banks that request for fixed monthly payments, merchant cash advances only deduct a small percentage from your credit/debit card sales monthly until your loan is repaid in full.

b. Business Loans

Business loans are non-traditional loans that make it easy for new investors and small businesses to have access to loans. However, the amount you will be able to access depends on your purpose and your business size.

c. Inventory Purchase Programs

This is another program that was set up to help small business and new investors. However, in inventory purchase programs, you are not given cash, rather basic expenses like inventory are given. This allows you to buy inventory at no upfront cost.

d. Family and Friends

Many people shy away from borrowing from their family and friends, but they could be your surest means of getting funds. When you borrow from your friends or family, you are meeting someone who knows you well and you are likely to get a loan with little or no interest.

However, it is important to note that it is important that all terms involving the loan are clearly stated so as to avoid dispute in the future.

Chapter 3: Myths About Money

Real estate investment has come under a lot of scrutinizing over the years. a lot of myths have been going around about accumulate and spending money in the industry. You cannot blame anyone that believes in those myths and the reason is simple. Some of these myths or misconception seem like common sense.

However, what has been evident is that, because these myths seem logical, they are not exactly correct. In fact, most of these myths have caused many real estate investors to lose out. Because they seem logical, you may be tempted to follow the advice and not think properly about the effects that they will have on your investment.

One of the biggest barriers of most people, both new and old real estate investor, in investing is money. It is not uncommon to find out that many leave their jobs for financial freedom in real estate investment. Maybe that is your motivation as well. So, money plays a huge role in investment and there are many myths and misconception about it.

If you will scale through as a new investor in real estate, then you must forgo these myths for they will do you more harm than good. let us address a few of these myths:

1. A lot of money is needed before you can start investing

Well, this is not exactly true as there are creative ways to finance. When you are buying a new property or taking a new mortgage, the truth is that it can be intimidating. You will definitely need the extra money that you likely don't have.

However, real estate investment is quite different from this. This is a form of generating passive income that will eventually pay for the cost of the property with time. And if you don't have the money, then you can always approach partners. Alternative financing and private money lenders are means you can use to get money for real estate investment.

The truth is this, the cost is involved and you should have money to cover for contingencies but you don't need to be rich to start investing in real estate.

2. You should focus on getting the cheapest properties you can find.

Cheap properties can be a good deal but they can as well be a nightmare. The truth is that most cheap properties come with lots of hidden problems you won't be aware of initially. When you get a property that seems cheap; watch out.

The issue is the cheap property may be good but the work required may be much. In other to make the property presentable, such property needs major fixes and what you will find out is that you will have to spend more time and money.

If the property is in a bad location, then you will also have a lot to lose. So, you see, cheap isn't always the real deal. You are likely to run into problems with the cheap property. And that isn't good for your cash flow. In the long run then, you will agree that you are not doing yourself any good by purchasing cheap properties.

3. You need to have good credit in other to invest in real estate

Here is another myth about money in real estate investment. The truth is that you don't need good credit to invest in real estate at all. You don't have to depend anymore on your credit in other to get access to funds to invest in real estate. Alternative financing such as private lending, partnering with other investors who have good credit are better options you can look towards.

You can also get involved in crowdfunding while you work on your credit. However, forget that you need to have good credit for you to invest in real estate. There are many real estate investors that are struggling with credit and limited resources, yet they are investing in real estate.

4. No matter what you do, you will lose money in the beginning

Again, this is not exactly true. You don't have to lose money if your calculated risk game is played right. There is risk in real estate but here is the good news; unlike gold prices or stocks, your investment is well within your control. You are not guessing or hoping that things will go well, you know it will.

However, there are cases where you make wrong decisions and the output lands you in problems, but that is part of your training and education. But also, the more you educate yourself, the more you have the equipping to take the calculated risk to succeed.

You must be thinking now that if it is possible not to lose money as a beginner. And the answer is that all you need to do is do your homework well and you will almost have a guaranty that no money will be lost.

5. Cutting costs should be your priority if you want to maximize your cash flow

You have got to be careful here. In the real estate business, frugality and smart money management are important. However, you don't want to cut cost at the expense of your property's long-term value.

Some real estate investors, especially the new ones, are fond of doing quick fixes that backfire. As much as possible, make sure you repair things the right way right from the first time even if it costs more. And if you need workers on your properties, make sure you go for quality and reliable people.

The point is this, in matters that count, don't cut corners. You need to know where cutting costs should be applied and when they should be not. Know them and you will do well in business.

The goal of investors in real estate is to make a profit, so it is not uncommon to find many issues around money. Some of these issues are the myths or misconceptions that have been ages long. In the end, you will find out that many of these misconceptions arose from the thoughts and ideas that were not thought through.

While we have examined these myths that surround investing in real estate and how to avoid them, don't you think it is only natural we begin to look into what to do to invest wisely and have the mindset of a millionaire investor? Well, let us do just that.

HOW TO DEVELOP THE MINDSET OF A MILLIONAIRE INVESTOR

Whether you realize it or not, financial wealth building is about personal growth. What you will find out is that if you will indeed by free financially, you have got to acquire new skills and great wisdom. It is also true that for you to enjoy the growth of your fortunes for long, you need to grow personally. And you will come to realize– if you haven't already- that financial freedom comes when you are free from working to live and you able to start living for your life's work.

In other to better understand how money works and how you can attain financial freedom, we must examine the mindset of millionaire real estate investors. We need to find out what they think about money, what their motivation for seeking financial wealth is and their understanding of it can be attained.

If you can fully grasp those, then you are in your way to freedom and you can begin your way to becoming a millionaire investor yourself.

For you to develop the mindset of a millionaire investor, you must first understand how other millionaire investors think and how they use their time. What you will find out, in the end, is that thinking is thinking.

Whether you are thinking big or small, it takes just about the same time and energy. The difference is often in the result that follows. So, whether you will think like a millionaire investor or not depends solely on you.

if you will scale through, you must pause and listen to the words of people who have gone ahead of you. Those who have worked this path and not only have they become millionaire investors really, but that also have attained financial freedom.

There are two major ways that are identified here that will make you have the mindset of a millionaire investor. Its time, let's examine these ways.

1. A Big Why

if you have been doing before, you should start now; follow the lives of successful people. Clip news articles, read biographies and watch documentation on their lives and what you should look out for is a pattern for achievement that is common to them all. I'm convinced without a doubt that you will discover that a strong will to succeed is simply what is common in them all.

All successful persons have been found out to have a compelling and personal reason to succeed. And that is what is called a Big Why. Motivation matters to be successful and it doesn't matter where it comes from.

This motivation comes from a different area and for various reasons. Some are quite interested in being successful out of a desire to be free from their jobs, achieve self-actualization or just have better choices in their life. They are powered by a Big Why.

If you be successful as well, then you have to follow in this footstep. Your life will be defined and redefined in ways you never imagine. However, to qualify as a Big Why, you need to have a motivation strong enough to propel you from the thinking phase to the acting phase. Here is a catch; once you are able to stop thinking about success as something you want to achieve and begin to feel it as something you not only need but also have to achieve, you will already be on your journey to success.

The question you need to ask yourself is if you are plugged into your Big Why. You also need to know if you are tapping into the energy it can bring to your life. Take a moment to reflect on what your biggest motivation is. Write down the things in your life that motivates you the most. Go beyond material goals. Write down your thoughts.

Hopefully, after carefully thinking through and taking your time, you will be able to write down that you are interested in financial wealth. One good thing about a Big Why is that it lets you have a clear focus. When you say yes to a thing, you are directly saying no to any other thing that can stand in the way of your success.

For instance, if you pursue financial freedom, you will know that excessive spending cannot be part of your attitude as it is against your long-term goal. A Big Why brings enormous stamina and incredible power to your financial focus. And, as you will find out, financial success requires that.

2. Think Big Goals

It is practically impossible to lead a big life without thinking big. In fact, what you will find out is that life is too big to think small. If you want to surpass your peers, and become a millionaire investor, you have got to think big. That is the fundamental key to winning.

Despite how important to think big, you will soon find out that it is in other to live a great life in reality, you must accompany your big thinking with big goals, big models and big habits. Without all these, your big thinking will be nothing more than wishful thinking.

All great people you can think of have a few things in common and partnering their thinking with actions is chief of those things. It then become unwise not to follow in the footstep of these great people who have taken the effort to clear the road and show the right path to breakthroughs.

As we have discussed in the previous point; how important the big why is. Understanding your big why gives you a picture of your destination, however the challenge lies in finding the bet path to get there. And that is where the Big Goals and the Big Models come in.

With the Big Goals intact, you are able to specifically restate what your Big Why is. And the Big Models are the steps and systems that will get you to those Big Goals. So, here is the point; an investor with a millionaire mindset has two objectives. The first is to establish the Big Goals and the other is to acquire Big Models.

You have got to be careful of short-term thinking though. For instance, if your goal is to have financial freedom, then you have got to state carefully what amount you intend to have at a certain time and how you plan to have that kind of money. The reason is because by the time you begin to find yourself in a better box from where you used to be, you begin to lose guard.

By the time you begin to follow the Big Models of Millionaire real estate investors, you will see that your daily activities will begin to look a lot like the high achievers.

Chapter 4: The Importance Of "Know-How" As Priority for The Success

Until a few years ago, the world of real estate investments was considered a market "for a few." You couldn't easily get into it unless you had large sums of money to invest and good knowledge. I myself, as a boy, had to do a lot of apprenticeship as a real estate agent to learn about the dynamics of this environment before starting my career, now over ten years, as a real estate investor. I can guarantee that it was not easy at the time. I have never had anyone teach me how to do it, so there was only one way to learn. Fortunately, today things have changed. The Internet is now within everyone's reach, and there is a lot of completely free material available for those entering this world

Could you ever become a perfect plumber by watching video tutorials on YouTube? You may be laughing at the trivial example, but the learning process is the same for every person, in any area. The answer to the question, however, is yes! But after how long and how many mistakes would you be able to call yourself a TRUE plumber? Probably after several years and in all sincerity, after all the mistakes you have made, I doubt that you will have the crowd of customers or construction companies that want to hire you, behind the door! Well, I can guarantee that the same thing also applies to the real estate investment sector. Some might even be able to close some profitable operations, if in possession of good sums to invest and with good knowledge, but without the help of a person who has already gone through it and many mistakes have already experienced them on their own skin, it becomes rather risky. The world of real estate investments is full of opportunities, but also of pitfalls; you need skills in different areas and if you don't pay attention by throwing yourself "blindly," you really risk losing your money (at best) or worse somebody else's money!

97% of investors fail or lose money in their investments.

Why? Simple, because almost everyone wants to earn a lot, in a short time, with the least possible effort and without having any kind of competence. REAL MONEY in this type of activity only comes AFTER the right training and AFTER a good dose of field experience. If you hope to get rich by staying on the sofa, you can go back to magical courses to get rich in two weeks without effort and without money.

MAKING REAL ESTATE INVESTMENTS IS ONE THING SERIOUS!

Do you want to know how it feels when you lose your money or worse, that of others? I felt these sensations on my skin when I started, unfortunately, without anyone telling me how to do it. I will never forget that period of my life, and I wouldn't wish for anything like this even to my worst enemy! The frustration of having worked for months without earning a dollar, indeed having lost many more, has spilled over into my way of working, my enthusiasm, and inevitably my private life. Not to mention the completely broken relationships with real estate agents, other professionals in the sector, and above all, with the equity partners who had invested with me.

Fortunately, those dark periods are over, and I currently have a team of professionals and investors all over with whom I have been making EXCLUSIVELY PROFIT investments for more than 30 years, and I have built an important portfolio of income properties that allows me to live on the income. All this, however, did not come without effort. Real success comes when you move to action after frequent learning.

Having a mentor to guide you along the way is the key to drastically speed up your results and avoid a lot of pain. Nobody should prove what I felt, not only for money but above all because our mistakes always have repercussions, inevitably on the people around us. I had no alternative to start my journey.

Now you can invest in a safe way, even if you don't have enough money after getting the right skills, everything comes easy because there will be someone who will show you the way, explaining the hidden pitfalls along the way and the skills that you absolutely must develop. Before starting a career full of personal and above all, economic rewards. These are the results of those who have decided to become a SAFE real estate investor,

For those who do not quite understand the essence of this process, we explain the materiel. An investment is the use of temporarily free cash in such a way that it makes a profit. In other words, real estate investments are investments in the purchase of residential or non-residential objects. It is assumed that as a result of such a purchase, the investor will increase his income or at least multiply the amount spent. At the same time, the purchased object must have high liquidity (the ability to quickly convert in monetary terms; in other words, it is the ability to quickly and expensively sell the object). The prospects for using the facility should also be bright. If all of the above conditions are met, it is considered that the investment experience is successful, and the goal is achieved.

Today, investing is an entire institution with a scientific justification and dozens of developed strategies. Using one of them, or developing your own, you can turn the usual amount of money into a source of constant income.

Chapter 5: Ways to Invest in Real Estate

WHERE TO START INVESTING

First of all, you need to have in hand the amount of money sufficient to invest in real estate. Why are loans and borrowings for these purposes a bad idea? Because it is difficult to guarantee a regular income from such investments. Concomitant expenses may also occur, and you already have a credit burden. It is optimal to have in stock all the amount necessary for investment. After you decide on the size of your investment, you must choose the area in which you want to receive income. In real estate, such areas are enough to make the choice that suits you and not to make a mistake. The concept of real estate includes many income categories. Investing in each of them has individual characteristics, and they are very diverse in terms of investor involvement and the amount of remuneration. We will deal with the main ones:

RESIDENTIAL INVESTMENT

Most potential investors are considering this option. It seems to them tempting and affordable. High constant income is drawn in thoughts, but costs? "Yes, there is no cost other than a purchase," they think. After all, the burden of paying communal services falls on the tenants of such apartments. And you know yourself, come for a profit once a month. In fact, the picture may be completely different. When considering residential real estate for investment, it is most practical to separate the concepts of primary and secondary housing. Each of them has its own characteristics when buying, selling. For these types of housing, different demand, respectively, and liquidity is also different.

Advantages of investments in housing in the secondary market:

- You get an apartment, ready for further actions, with decoration and more;

- You can rent an apartment. Tenants will pay most of the costs associated with the maintenance of the apartment;
- An apartment can be quickly and profitably sold if necessary. And almost certainly you will be in the plus to what you spent on the purchase;
- You can make a tax refund of part of the spent amount, which can also be a pleasant bonus to income.

Cons of investing in finished housing:

- The market is oversaturated, finding residents is not easy;
- Finding solvent tenants is even more difficult;
- To rent housing, it is necessary to purchase furniture and household appliances;
- Tenants can damage the interior of the apartment, and again have to make repairs or purchase furniture;
- Many prefer to buy new apartments;
- Due to external factors and the abundance of new buildings, the cost of housing in the secondary market may fall significantly over the years;
- If you do not plan to rent the purchased apartment, then you will have to pay taxes, fees, and utility bills yourself. However, you will pay the real estate tax in any case, regardless of the presence or absence of tenants.

INVESTING IN RESIDENTIAL PROPERTY

As for housing in the primary market, you can choose different strategies for investing in it. One of them is the purchase of housing at the excavation stage. A very profitable, but at the same time, very risky investment. It all depends on the integrity of the developer.

Pros:

- At the stage of excavation, the cost of apartments is much lower than their completed counterparts;

- According to the results of the construction, you get a completely new apartment.

Cons:

- The developer can go broke, lose the license and just run away with your money long before the end of construction;
- If the apartment is rented out, you still have to repair and finish. And this is also a cost;
- You do not receive any dividends until the end of construction.

The second option is to conclude an agreement on shared participation in the construction and buy an apartment in a house of a high degree of readiness. These investments differ from the purchase at the stage of excavation. Some risks increase, some, on the contrary, go away.

PROS OF BUYING A HOME IN A NEW BUILDING:

- When buying an apartment in a house with a high degree of readiness, there is a greater chance of waiting for the soon completion of construction and putting the house into operation;
- An apartment will cost a little cheaper than a similar one in houses that are already rented out, but more expensive than those that have not yet been built.

Cons of buying a home in a new building:

- There are risks of problems for the developer and delays in the completion of construction;
- If you bought an apartment from the developer for resale in the future, the status of housing will change from "primary" to "secondary." And many are eager to buy housing in the primary market since this procedure provides for preferential mortgages and the possibility of applying for a tax deduction for home decoration. Accordingly, the circle of potential buyers will be substantially narrower.

- In order to benefit from the purchased apartment, before buying, it is worth exploring some related conditions. The liquidity of the property, tenant demand, and price growth (or fall) over the years will depend on them:
- The apartment should be located in a good area (environmentally friendly, accessible from the point of view of transport, saturated with the necessary infrastructure).
- The apartment should be conveniently planned (the presence of a balcony or loggia, not angular, not on the top floor, separate rooms, and a bathroom, a decent area of the kitchen).
- The apartment should have a fresh repair, and preferably a beautiful view from the window. Corner apartments are also not considered a very good option.

COMMERCIAL REAL ESTATE INVESTMENT

These are buildings and premises in which you can place warehouses, offices, trading floors, beauty salons, and so on. Entrance to this market is much more expensive than when buying a residential apartment. But the income received can be much higher. Firms and industrial organizations are actively growing and developing in the country. And they will always need rooms for comfortable work. Not every entrepreneur can buy an office or warehouse, but renting such premises is within the power of everyone who needs them and is doing business.

COMMERCIAL INVESTMENT

Pros for renting commercial real estate:

- High demand for office and warehouse space;
- Higher rental income compared to residential apartments;
- The tenant independently equips the premises to his needs.

Cons of renting commercial real estate:

- High tax on non-residential premises;
- Significant initial investment;

- The possibility of long downtime of the property
- The need to hire an accountant in order to deal with the financial side of the issue. You must correctly calculate and pay tax on rental income.

PROPERTY LOCATED OUTSIDE THE CITY (COUNTRY AND VILLAGE HOUSES)

As a tool for obtaining real investment, income is rather weak. If a country house is purchased for subsequent rental, then you need to be aware of some features of working with this type of real estate. For example, finding a family for permanent year-round living in a country house is not a quick matter. Alternatively, you can rent a country house for holidays, but this also requires some advertising and activity. Therefore, the advantages regarding the first two types of investments are small, and the minuses are more significant.

Investment in suburban real estate

Pros:

Low cost of investments;

Low property tax due to the fact that the object is outside the city limits.

Cons:

- There is no guarantee of a stable income. In general, there are none of them for any type of investment, but country houses are favorites in this regard.
- It is necessary that the country house be equipped with all the attributes necessary for living and celebrations;
- In the absence of tenants, the house in the winter must still be heated and monitored (robbers often hunt in summer cottages);
- For a profitable rental, transport accessibility is required - both public transport and personal. That is, the roads and access to the house must be in good condition.

Of course, over time, a purchased house can grow in price, and then the investor will still remain in positive territory when selling property. But there are still risks to lose property that is far away without the ability to control it. For example, a fire may occur. The authorities may decide to lay a highway through the holiday village and withdraw the land for state needs. Or organize a landfill in some meters away, and then the acquisition will depreciate sharply. Therefore, real estate removed from the owner is a rather shaky investment.

INVESTMENTS IN THE HOTEL BUSINESS

Some creative investors are considering investing in the hotel business. No, we do not mean buying a stake in a chain of famous hotels (although this is also an investment). We mean the purchase of residential real estate (houses or apartments) and the conversion into small rooms for short stays. This type of business is widely developed in our resort cities. And in the capital, it's a sin to hide, and hostels are in demand.

HOSPITALITY INVESTMENTS

Pros:

High profitability due to the constant flow of customers;

For a good profit is not necessary, So that all beds are constantly occupied;

Cons: High cost of acquiring real estate. Since the arrangement of hotels and hostels is prohibited by law in residential apartments, you will have to transfer the apartment to non-residential status or immediately buy commercial property;

- High investments in good repairs and in the purchase of necessary furniture;
- Maintaining the internal situation at the proper level;
- Active advertising so that as many places as possible are constantly occupied;
- It is necessary to register the individual entrepreneur and bear all the costs associated with this — financial statements, taxes, and so on.
- Investing in real estate abroad
- There is a certain proportion of investors who consider buying an apartment in other states a good investment, generating considerable income. Currently, this type of activity is actively developing.

FOREIGN INVESTMENT

Pros:

- in some countries during the holiday season you can get high income from renting out real estate;
- part of the property can be rented all year round;
- You can get passive income by concluding an agreement with a real estate agency. The company will look for tenants and deal with their settlement. You will be transferred part of the rent. The real estate agent will leave the rest for itself. Income under this scheme is quite high;
- wide range of financial investments. You can purchase both an apartment and a villa. Depending on the planned size of the investment.

Cons:

- Not in every country is real estate available for sale to foreign nationals;
- To understand what is happening, you must be fluent in at least English. It is best to know the language of the country in which the purchase is planned;
- You do not understand the legal intricacies of another state. To do this, you will have to hire a lawyer or still carefully study the language;
- At least once you have to visit this country. And plan all the expenses associated with the trip - visa, flight, accommodation, and so on.

LAND

They also relate to real estate and may be sold, bought, and leased.

Pros:

- speed of execution
- low cost (relative to real estate);
- lack of need for repair and utilities;

- You can make a deal without involving intermediaries due to the simplicity of registration.

Cons:

- After the purchase, the land must be used for its intended purpose, and this is an additional cost (agricultural processing, construction of a house, etc.);
- The land tax has recently grown and plans to grow yet.
- Buying parking spaces
- A very profitable investment for residents of megacities. Parking spaces in new buildings scatter like hotcakes. The stream of people wishing to rent a parking space in the house will never run dry. All investments will pay off in a short period of time. True, some developers sell parking spaces only to owners of apartments in the house. But if you bought an apartment in a new building and you still have a certain amount of money, buy a couple more parking spaces than you need. This will provide you with constant passive income. At the same time, additional expenses in this type of activity are not needed.

The problem is that FII is not a fixed income. In the event of an economic, financial, or real estate crisis, it is better to have physical property in your name than shares in a fund managed by a third party. You can even invest directly in real estate. You can form a group of friends and relatives to undertake in this sector. Even with real estate bubble rumors, you need to be prepared to go shopping when prices drop. Downturns generate great buying opportunities. Real estate investment gives numerous leverage and opportunities for investment for investors to pick from.

1. Invest in land

They are great generators of wealth. Investing in land in the vicinity of large capitals is a guaranteed value in the long run. This is because cities are expanding horizontally at an accelerated pace. There are also several ways to invest and profit from land in the short and medium-term. Many luxury condominiums are built in real swamps, flooded land around ponds that would have no value in the eyes of an ordinary person.

2. Invest in real estate in the plant

In the last four years, many people bought real estate in the plant paying only 20% to 30% of its value to resell them 1 or 2 years after the beginning of the works with enormous gains. This is possible with the use of the technique that allows multiplying the profitability through indebtedness. It is necessary to know how to evaluate the property correctly. Not every property in the plant is really advantageous when it is intended to sell it before handing over the keys to profit from the premium.

3. Invest in used real estate

It is in the mud that we find the diamonds. Right now, thousands of used properties are stranded in real estate. They are apartments and houses despised by the final consumer. The prepared investor is able to identify these opportunities, polish these properties, and then sell them with huge returns in the short term.

4. Invest in rental properties

The secret of the lease is in the correct choice of properties. There are great opportunities in different segments, such as popular properties, flats, commercial rooms, stores, warehouses, vacation homes, and hotels. It is important to know each of these businesses. The best rental investment option may depend on the characteristics of the city where you live and your investor profile.

5. Build real estate to sell or rent

Here we have another machine to multiply assets. When you buy a finished property, you are paying the cost of construction and the profit of whoever built it. And believe me, this profit is absurdly high. I know a small merchant who, before retiring, bought land in a poor neighborhood in the city. He built a 3-story property with nine small apartments. He invested $500 thousand in the land and the work.

Before the works were finished, I had already rented the nine apartments for $560 each. He achieved a great retirement. The investment guarantees a return greater than 1% per month, and the building is now worth more than $1 million. This type of investment is widely practiced by investors.

6. Invest safely

Investing in real estate can be risky if you don't invest in knowledge first. Buying a property is not like buying a car at a dealership. Large companies in the market are involved in cases of disrespect to the consumer. And what most generates these problems is the lack of information. Nowadays, it is cheap to buy information, and you just don't get information before investing who doesn't want to.

7. The value of a property depends on its use

There are many properties near you that are being underutilized. There are residential properties that are bad investments if they are purchased for residential use and great if they are turned into commercial properties. The opposite situation can also happen. The informed and prepared investor is able to identify this type of opportunity that is difficult for the average consumer to perceive.

8. Investing with little money is possible

You don't need to have a lot of money to invest in real estate. There are even those who invest without having any money through real estate financed and acquired through a consortium. The use of leverage in the acquisition of lots within condominiums and properties in the plant are great strategies to diversify your investments in immobilizing a lot of money.

9. Investing using reason, not emotion

While most people buy real estate emotionally, driven by impulse, visual, and sentimental appeals, the investor works rationally. Turning overgrown land into a piece of paradise is the specialty of investors. For a prepared investor, there is no bad property, no matter if it is inside a slum or in the most upscale neighborhood in the city. A good investment property doesn't have to be beautiful and well located; it needs to make a profit.

10. Form an investment group

Do you have a lawyer friend? Do you have another friend who is an engineer or an architect? Do you understand finance? Why don't you get your friends together and create your own real estate investment fund? Together, you are big, and in the real estate market, this makes a difference. There are groups of friends who come together to buy entire businesses at a bargain price due to their bargaining power. Others prefer to come together to build and then rent. Many subdivisions, commercial buildings, and housing developments are the result of investments by small investors. How many opportunities have you missed in your city in recent years due to a lack of knowledge?

Chapter 6: How to Develop Sound Criteria for Identifying Great Real Estate Investment Opportunities

The number of new investors who discover all the benefits of the real estate market and wish to invest their money in a safe and profitable way is very large. However, knowing how to differentiate promising businesses becomes a big challenge.

When analyzing the proposals that exist in the market, you can come across a multitude of different properties: apartments on the floor with modern proposals, university properties, houses in tourist cities, old properties that need renovation, among many others. And, even analyzing properties with the same characteristic, it is possible to find the most diverse values and particularities. With all this universe of possibilities, making a decision on where to invest the money creates a lot of insecurity. After all, you want to make sure you are really investing your money in an investment that can generate good returns in the future, don't you?

COMPARE THE PRICE OF THE PROPERTY

The first factor analyzed to identify a good real estate investment opportunity should be the price of the property. This will be the biggest expense of your investment, and all the revenue generated from the rental or sale of this property will be used to recover the initial investment. That is, saving at the time of purchase can dramatically increase the profitability of the operation.

Imagine that you are monitoring the prices of real estate in a region and discover an apartment that is 10% cheaper than the others because the real estate company has an urgency to get the cash value. In this situation, this 10% savings can directly reflect the return on investment of the operation.

But how do you know that a property is priced well? The secret is to do good research and constantly monitor the values of the properties in the region in which you want to invest. Instead of buying a property in the first week of research, you can spend two months just analyzing. After that period, you will surely know when a property is priced well.

ANALYZE OTHER REAL ESTATE INVESTMENT SPENDING

Don't be fooled: the value of the property is the biggest expense of your investment, but it is far from being the only expense. After the purchase of the property, you will still need to face costs with the registration of the property, taxes, maintenance, cleaning, among others. These expenses also need to be included in your planning to analyze the profitability that real estate investment can generate.

This is an analysis that becomes even more important when you buy a property that has years of use. In such cases, it is very likely that you will have a lot of expenses with repairs and maintenance to leave the place in excellent condition to be rented or sold.

ASSESS THE REGION'S APPRECIATION POTENTIAL

Price is undoubtedly an essential aspect in determining a real estate investment opportunity. But the potential for property appreciation maybe even more important in the profitability generated by an operation in the real estate market.

It is possible that there are two properties that cost R $ 350 thousand in different regions of the city. While one of them suffers a small devaluation over the years, the other may be worth R $ 400 thousand after two years. In other words, the initial price was the same, but the profitability of the operation certainly varies widely.

This is precisely why real estate investors need to keep an eye on regions that have a good prospect of appreciation - with the emergence of new developments, greater public circulation, improved infrastructure, among other factors. On the other hand, it is also necessary to pay attention to regions that are beginning to show signs of devaluation.

ALIGN YOUR GOALS

A good real estate investment opportunity for you may not be seen as a good opportunity for another investor. As promising as the conditions may be, you need to take into account what your goals are before applying for your money.

This is an issue that deserves your attention because of the risks you run when running away from your goal. If you want a rental property with long-term contracts but end up buying a more profitable property with short-term rentals, it will be essential that you have a much longer time available to serve all visitors - and disorganization can compromise income generated.

SEEK INFORMATION ABOUT THE PUBLIC

Imagine that you find a four-bedroom apartment with very attractive prices - even costing less than the other three-bedroom properties. After closing the purchase of this property, you decide to make it available for rental. However, several months go by without you being able to find many interested parties.

It is necessary to consider that a four-bedroom apartment has a lower demand than one, two, or three-bedroom apartments. Depending on the region in which it is located, the demand for such large properties can be very low. Thus, an investment that seemed very promising turns into a major headache.

Before you even start your real estate investment, it is essential that you gather information about the public that may be interested in your lease or purchase in the future. The more the property is able to satisfy the needs of the public, the easier it will be to close good deals - with the possibility of increasing the amount charged.

CALCULATE THE FEASIBILITY OF FINANCING

For investors who opt for financing at the time of purchase, it is also important to accurately calculate all expenses that will be generated over the years. After all, the payment of monthly installments consumes the return generated by the investment. The financial issue is always of great importance in determining a good real estate investment opportunity.

Chapter 7: How to Attract Private Money Lenders and Partners

Often aspiring real estate investors complain of a lack of funds as a real estate startup. I was lucky because I started with a small capital that allowed me to do the first operation of a studio apartment. After having had this property, I got a mortgage and then liquidity, and from there I started to finance my operations, so there was a process in which I was a bit luckier than those who do not have immediate availability. So, let's see what the three ways to be financed in your business as a real estate investor are:

Credit institutions: It is the easiest way because when you need money, you go to the bank to ask for it, however not all banks finance any people. For example, if one goes to the bank and asks for a loan to operate in the real estate sector and is denied, so the person puts his soul in peace. In reality, lenders prefer to finance certain categories of people, some employees, other professionals, and there are lenders that have different policies. A credit broker who knows the lenders and can help you in the search for capital can help you in this.

Relatives and friends: I also used this lever in the past with very close parents or relatives. If you have relatives who can support you, this is a way to get funding.

Capital investors: I have been working exclusively with them for several years. They are people with the capital in the bank who do not make it enough and want to approach the world of real estate investments but do not have time or skills, for example. A doctor or dentist. The formula that I have personally found is very practical and convenient: I have chosen to work with a capital investor only, so if I have to do a 100 thousand dollar operation, I choose a single capital investor who can invest them, and it will be the person who will property. If he accepts the proposal that I will make, it will always be a discount property, he will buy the property and pay for the renovation, and I, as a consultant, follow all the steps, and he deducts the interventions made. When a buyer buys the property, it will always be the capital investor to cash the amount. There remains a net profit figure that is divided between him and me who carried out the operation and issue an invoice for advice. This is a policy that I like a lot, but how can we get there? I currently have a waiting list of people who have given me capital, but I can't satisfy them all. To get to this point you must be a real estate investor with real practice, and then you must first use the two previous items, record the activities you carry out and create your own online presence, in this way investors will see that in a continuous way places are contained in which you show your business. If you want to attract capital investors, the process is long, and you have to start it right away.

Obviously, you need to have sufficient capital or, better yet, you must be able to get financed by the banks: First of all, a premise is needed. It is, in fact, essential to distinguish between those who want to buy a new house to live there, alone, as a couple, or together with their family and those who want to buy a property to invest their money, perhaps reselling it, once renovated to a higher price, or even to look for a guaranteed monthly fixed income to count on, such as that which clearly could derive from a rent. It is clear that these are two very different types of purchases, which, as such, imply different strategies.

There is an orientation of we no longer have access to credit today, but this is a lie. The money is still there for everyone, just knowing how to ask it correctly, getting the right information and the right channel for lending the money is a very important tool in investment. Managing to find the best rates and the best credit opportunities evaluating each time different lenders and various proposals is a major key to the success of a real estate agent.

Obviously, needless to say, banks and real estate investments go hand in hand: in general, anyone who wishes to invest in real estate needs financing, and even those who have their own capital have greater convenience in borrowing at least a part of the capital they need for the operation. That he has in mind, let's see, together with to understand what it is essential to know and what you must necessarily prepare before going to the bank to ask for money, if you really want to have a chance to be able to get funded on the project you have in mind.

SOME SIMPLE RULES FOR THOSE WHO WANT TO INVEST AND NEED CREDIT FROM BANKS

1- Anyone wishing to invest must demonstrate that they are expert in their area and sector

First, those who want to make real estate investments must inevitably be, or become, "expert" in your area: every place has its peculiarities and its customers, which manifests specific requirements. In each place, there are different dynamics for what concerns the real estate market, and it is essential to know them thoroughly to think about investing and earning!

The experience of the area is therefore strategic, also from a bank credit point of view. If it is necessary to understand exactly where you want to invest, it is equally important to know how the area and the credit market of your area move. However, a real estate career cannot be created overnight. The most important thing for a property developer is to be a real professional in the sector: to be able to get credit from the banks, you can't improvise!

Anything to be well done must be carried out with the necessary skills by expert and qualified people.

2-Preparing a detailed and truthful business plan is fundamental

Up to here, it is all theory but, surely you are wondering: in practice, what do I need to be able to get credit from banks? Undoubtedly the basic tool and also the easiest to use, the one we have always used for all our investments, as well as for the last one is the Business Plan. Within this document, in a certain sense, you have to tell your idea, convincing the reader that it is a winning and safe investment, as it is well thought out in all its aspects.

But what can't be missing from a business plan?

Who we are

First of all, you need to introduce yourself, declare who it is that intends to do the real estate operation, or explain who you are, what you do, where you come from, what is your experience in the field, as well as that of the companies you intend to involve in the operation that you propose. Banks no longer look only at guarantees (now they are full of properties they own which they don't know what to do with them!), They are the first to want the operation to be successful, and for this reason, they rely heavily on the personal and working history of the single entrepreneur who goes to apply for a loan.

Your experience, your history, your businesses speak for you; facts matter more than words! For this reason, I would not advise a novice to start big by building from scratch on a building plot. The credibility of the company and people is essential and must be built day by day.

Here, then, in the Business Plan, you will have to illustrate all the elements that distinguish your company, specifying well what your uniqueness is, what makes you different from the others.

For example, I am the property developer with the heart, and everything revolves around the house for me, the house with the heart, even my business card is in the shape of a house. Obviously, it is certainly not the note that makes the difference, but it is many things together that distinguish me in the territory in which I operate: your Brand, your history, and your uniqueness are essential.

WHY WE WANT TO DO OWN THAT DETERMINED REAL ESTATE OPERATION

Secondly, of course, you will have to explain the reasons that led you to choose precisely that type of real estate transaction: because you have chosen that particular area, because of that area rather than another, because of precisely that property!

In this regard, it is very important, upstream, to carry out an accurate market investigation. Remember that you are not going to build your dream house: do not think about how and where you would like it! You have to make another person's dream come true, but to do it you must first understand if what you think you can achieve can really be someone else's dream if there is someone who is inside your target and to do so it is essential to know exactly what the wishes of those who live or would like to go to live in that particular place are.

This is done with an investigation of the area: you have to look around, see what's around, what are the most popular types of housing, what other construction sites are nearby, what cuts they propose, what technologies they use and of course what is the average price per square meter of that area. Only in this way can you realize if what you thought you were offering is already present and if it is something you like, or if on the contrary, destined for the same target, there is already something unsold around. Needless to think of building studios in an area mainly inhabited by families, as well as in an area where students or singles live, small villas and apartments are more complex to sell!

WHICH BANK? EYE OF CHOICE!

Ideas don't matter to banks: they only care about data, numbers! Today, in fact, although the market is recovering, access to construction credit is tough! So, more than in any other field, it is good to know what you are doing, and you must start, at least, armed with the best conditions. Another thing to keep in mind: not all banks can get credit, every institution is different! So how do you do it? You need to have a deep knowledge of the area, not only in real estate terms but also in terms of credit, to choose an institution that has certain characteristics: exactly what you are looking for!

Remember, however, that today, any bank manages to have all your data available; therefore, it is not at all wise to play on the numbers and try to get the accounts back in some way, what you write in the Business Plan must be real and refutable. There are slower, more cumbersome institutions, with which it is more difficult to dialogue and work, also because for company policy it is already known, a priori, that they do not like to invest in the real estate sector, then it will also be useless to waste time consulting them!

In the real estate sector, timeliness is very important. Therefore, you must be able to choose a local partner, interested and fast! The supreme purpose of any real estate investment, of course, is to create profitability from the operation, and the bank must be clear that this profit margin exists and must be clearly quantified.

THE ALTERNATIVES: WHY OWN THIS INVESTMENT?

The Business Plan must be used to remove any doubts from the bank about the investment you intend to make and must be able to answer what might be the questions, doubts, concerns, and objections in this regard, without even having to manifest them. Obviously, everything must be clearly documented !!! No theory, only practice, and real numbers!!!

At one time, lenders looked only at the guarantees you were able to offer them; today instead of guarantees (which are still important, but no longer so fundamental), the bank cares to be sure of getting back the money lent. The fact of being able to have a mortgage on a property does not interest him! Currently, banks have so many properties owned by mortgages that they can't resell, and they don't know what to do with them, that they certainly don't want more! Never before has the bank bet with the real estate agent and only does so if he has a good margin of certainty, of course!

3- IN ADDITION TO THE BUSINESS PLAN, A PRECISE TIME PLAN IS ALSO NEEDED

Clearly, in addition to the Business Plan, it is essential to have clear ideas also as regards the logistical and shipbuilding aspect of the work. It is essential to set a start date and, at the same time, an end date. The timeline is very important because, in fact, it allows the bank to know when it can get its money back!

It is, therefore, necessary to make a prediction and draw up a fairly precise time schedule of the works. Be careful to always keep in mind that a whole series of unexpected events can happen to you. In real estate transactions, unexpected events, more or less numerous and more or less large, unfortunately always occur, starting from the moment you buy a land or a property to be redeveloped until the sale of the finished apartments and sometimes even afterward. Here too, the ideal would always be to be able to conclude the real estate transaction in conjunction with the end of the construction site, selling everything on paper, but today it is not that simple! When buying a house, there is a lot of money at stake, and people are afraid and do not want to risk, even if today there are bank and insurance guarantees to guarantee the buyer and Law 210 goes to protect compromise and deposits!

4. The SWOT analysis

After the timeline, it is essential to face the so-called SWOT analysis. It is a strategic planning tool used to evaluate the strengths (Strengths), the weaknesses (Weaknesses), the opportunities (Opportunities) and the risks and threats (Threats) connected to the realization of a specific project, or to actually understand what can separate us from the achievement of the goal we have set ourselves. This analysis serves to acquire the awareness necessary for really know what you're up against. Only in this way can you be aware of any risks associated with the investment, and you can, even before they occur, think about how to deal with them without being caught unprepared and having the necessary resources to stem them. Do not delude yourself: in a real estate operation, there are always risks; it's never all roses and flowers; the important thing, however, is to have them clearly in mind and already know how to cope with them, without panicking!

5- PRESENTING YOURSELF WITH A TEAM AND A PROJECT ALREADY WELL DEFINED

Of course, the bank must also present concrete projects, and you must make it clear that you are the first to really believe in the operation you are proposing and that you believe it to such an extent that you have already started investing your capital in person, hiring a team of designers who have already produced a preliminary project, which then will clearly be refined, but which in its being already fully outlines what the final result wants to be. The bank wants to know who will take care of the project, the execution of the works, the direction of the same, the supply of materials, and so on.

6- IN THE END IT IS THE NUMBERS THAT COUNT

In the end, what matters and what really matters to the bank are the numbers. It is essential to present a clear financial and economic plan which shows how much the operation you are proposing allows you to earn, both for you and the bank. To do this, it is necessary to quantify in a precise way what are the real costs necessary for the realization of the work and if and how much you earn.

Without a careful analysis of the operation, you intend to carry out, accompanied by a well-made Business Plan, it is not possible to ask anyone for anything. Even so, it is not at all said that you still manage to get credit from the bank, but without knowledge of the facts, no one will give you, not only credit but not even listening!

Relationship with credit institutions has definitely improved, certainly also because you need to be clear and sincere with the banks and investors, never lie about your real intentions, nor ever be overly optimistic forecasts, already knowing a priori that the profit would have been lower than expected.

Chapter 8: The Ugly Side of Creative Investing

Real estate funds are very attractive to investors due to the many advantages they offer, especially due to the wide diversification capacity that this category of investments offers, in addition to also providing investment strategies of different modalities (capital gain, income, diversification, etc.) all of them directed to the real estate sector.

Among the main advantages, therefore,

Dilution of risks: A real estate fund can invest in several projects, thereby dividing the financial capacity of the properties' income and spreading possible financial risks;

Equity succession: Agility of succession due to the fractioning in shares of the accumulated equity;

Portfolio diversification: Through a real estate fund, it is possible to invest in properties with lower investment volumes when compared to direct investment in properties in the traditional market;

Good governance (in general): FIIs have specialized managements, which are responsible for the fund's real estate strategies. This means less bureaucracy for investors;

Property protection: Mitigation of tax and labor risks existing in the SPE structure;

Quota liquidity: While the purchase process for selling real estate in the traditional market may take months to complete, it is possible to negotiate thousands of reais per day in the secondary market for real estate funds, depending on the FII;

However, like everything else in life, there is also the other side of the coin; that is, there are important points of attention that need to be taken into account by investors.

Among the main disadvantages, therefore, it is worth mentioning here:

Absence of guarantees: Once acquired by the FII, the properties cannot be mortgaged or pledged as collateral to obtain financing and other forms of fundraising;

Absence of ownership and unavailability of assets: Quotas of real estate funds do not confer ownership of properties. Shareholders cannot dispose of the assets that make up the real estate fund's assets;

Limited decision-making capacity: Shareholders are unable, individually, to make the purchase and/or sale decisions on assets, this decision being made by the management of funds, in the vast majority of cases;

Quota volatility: Although it is much less than that of stocks, the volatility of quotas of real estate funds can cause some discomfort to investors, especially beginners;

Closed condominium: The redemption of shares of a real estate fund is not allowed. The exit of the investment, therefore, must be made through the negotiation of shares in the secondary market, or with an eventual liquidation of the FII;

Given the above, it is up to you, the investor, to put the advantages on the scale, on the one hand, the advantages, and on the other, the disadvantages, to decide which weight has an advantage in the comparison.

Of course, our opinion can be seen as somewhat partisan, but we have the slight impression that the advantages side tends to be "a little" more representative than the disadvantages of real estate funds.

Chapter 9: How to Get Started with No Money or Experience

Starting a new career is not easy. There is a lot to learn, and the desire to get immediate results can lead to making the normal beginner's mistakes. As a real estate agent, you are helping your client in the process of buying or selling a home. It is very easy to be emotionally connected to the transition of the property and let the process become personal. Remember before and during the process that "It's not about me ... I have a home!" in order to make the journey easier and better for you as a beginner in the field of real estate, and you need to discover and learn from a mentor. There is no way to learn from a person who has known the real estate business for tens of years. It is the best way to shorten the learning curve. As clever as it is, experience counts for a lot. See how your mentor contacts customers, visits, prepares and organizes workflow, and, most importantly, sell or raises a property. Anything you can learn with help will result in better use of your time. The best part of our job is that we don't have anyone telling us what to do and when to do it. As a result, we may not do enough for the salary at the end of the month to be reasonable. Make a schedule to help you get organized to get into the habit of doing multiple tasks in one day, without wasting time thinking about what you have to do. Don't let your schedule be dictated by the casualness of the events. Define blocks of time with essential activities that you will have to complete. Time to raise, time to promote properties, time to create your personal brand. Real estate agents with no experience will have to dedicate a lot of time, at the beginning of their careers, to raising and creating a brand identity, which will distinguish them from other professionals.

It seems easy, but few real estate agents do everything they can. If you tell a client, a potential client, or another real estate agent that you are going to do something, DO IT! By law, we are required to have the training, but sometimes the lack of time does not help. The world we live in is constantly changing, and the way business is managed also changes. We should be aware of new legislation, new technologies, marketing, naming just a few. Change is our only constant. If we are not aware, we are left behind.

Good business practice is to meet with buyers and sellers to explain the process of buying or selling a property. However, real estate agents are so eager to negotiate that they sometimes forget to explain the whole process in detail, how it works, and what is expected from the client. Manage expectations from the first meeting so that you can maintain a minimum stress level throughout the transaction.

When you go to the office, treat yourself like a professional, you never know who might arrive looking for an agent. When you are in an open house, get to know the neighborhood, what has been sold recently, and what is also available for the market. Always keep your material with you, you never know when a potential customer appears, you won't want to walk around to compile the information

Regardless of training, the real estate market makes room for anyone who wants to be a broker. From graduates in diverse areas to young professionals and even retirees, the sector has professional brokers from different origins, from engineers to lawyers working in the field. The reasons are the most varied: flexibility in working hours, the possibility of greater financial gains, and improvement in the quality of life. Another fact that has attracted people to the career of real estate is the unusual growth of the real estate market. If you want to turn your life around and take a good look at the career of a realtor, it's good to get ready! Since nothing in this life resolves overnight, you need to complete a few steps before selling your first home. It is worth remembering that it is essential that it starts in partnership with a company that has easy traffic in the market, and that "opens doors" for you. A card with a strong name is the solid foundation you need for a successful partnership.

This company must have a reliable and abundant database, as well as management tools that facilitate quick adaptation to the new business.

To start your career right, you need to partner with a company with a strong background. This company must have a reliable and abundant database, as well as management tools that facilitate quick adaptation to the new business—anyway, the Training course. Yes, you have to get a diploma to enter this field. The training can be done at the Faculty of Science Real Estate, lasting four years, or in the course of Real Estate Management, done in 2 years. There is a shorter path: take the Real Estate Transition Technician course that lasts 4 to 18 months, depending on the school. Well, that you should already know, as it is for any career, but research the most respected schools and colleges in the market and confirm their legality with the Ministry of Education. That, too, makes a difference. Phase The best faculty is life and work. Nothing better than putting into practice everything you see in your course. Take advantage of this internship moment to observe how the market works and to build your own way of trading. It is common for some educational institutions to nominate students for internships. But, if that doesn't happen, look for real estate agents operating in your region, where you are already familiar. In order not to be just another one in the middle, it is important to look for extra courses to complement your training. Knowledge in Real Estate Law, for example, is essential to build a transparent career.

HOW DO YOU INVEST WITHOUT MONEY IN REAL ESTATE?

Real estate investment must be made with leverage. If you want to make an investment only with your money, you have not understood the essence of the real estate investment. That is precisely the possibility of investing with money that is not yours, that is, leverage.

There are various techniques for investing in real estate without putting up your capital.

The classic method is to make a mortgage or involve financial partners.

The Transfer of Compromise is a completely legal practice. In practice, it consists of selling a property before it has definitively become your property at a higher price than that agreed with the owner. The gain is all in the difference in price, which we will be able to tear thanks to minimal improvements made to the property. There is no need to invest capital in this type of operation, or at the maximum, the amount required is really minimal, but the ROI of this type of operation is very high.

The Excerpts instead consist of buying a property before it goes to auction, intervening in a real estate execution procedure, establishing an agreement with the debtor and creditors to pay off the debts, extinguish the procedure and thus prevent the property from being sold to the auction. The property can be resold before the signing of the deed to a third party at market price, but with the excerpts, you can buy properties at least 50% off!

SHOULD YOU INVEST IN REAL ESTATE IN THIS TIME OF CRISIS?

This is an optimal time to make money with real estate. Today the market belongs to buyers, so today we do business that 1-2 years ago could not be done. Today it is possibly more difficult to sell (but it depends on the city, the size, the price, and the goodness of the deal). Rule N.1 of real estate investment becomes even more important: money is made when buying.

WELL AND SCRATCHES BADLY?

The question often asked by skeptics is: why do you spend time being a trainer if the techniques you say you know are so rewarding?

In fact, I have found 22 companies operating in various sectors so far: from luxury car rental to real estate excerpts, to the manufacture of industrial fabrics. Training is one of these activities, which engages the weekend and gives me a lot of satisfaction. I need the contact of the people, the comparison, to feel that what the experience I have accumulated can also serve someone else.

DO YOU HAVE A TIP FOR REAL ESTATE AGENTS IN THIS DELICATE PHASE FOR THE SECTOR?

Consider other innovative forms of buying and selling: rent-to-buy (American technique that allows you to rent before buying, to "try the house") or home staging, that is, proposing settings that allow the potential customer to appreciate the potential of the property, thus improving negotiations.

CAN YOUR COURSES BE USEFUL FOR REAL ESTATE AGENTS?

In my courses, I have already met hundreds of real estate agents. They were fascinated by the buying and selling techniques that I explain because they can significantly increase the number of transactions made and increase their turnover. Not to mention the improvement in the quality of the service provided to the customer, which can be accompanied and recommended in situations other than the classic sale. However, it is necessary that the agent has the entrepreneurial mentality or the perspective of becoming an entrepreneur and not the mediator's approach.

Do you think the real estate market will rise?

As always, the market has had some ups and downs. The important question is not whether the average transaction price will go up or down. Rather, the important question is: will there be more transactions during the following here. This is an important fact. I think so, given that banks are gradually "reopening the taps" of credit.

HOME SALES CLOSING TECHNIQUES

When starting out as a real estate investor, you need to understand some basic techniques to put you on track when you try to close your first deal;

1. Develop a trusting relationship with the customer

For consumers to buy your product, it is essential that they trust you. This implies working with honesty and transparency and in the most spontaneous way possible. It is easier to trust a spontaneous salesman than a salesman who is suspicious or who proves to be doubtful. That is the type who seems more interested in earning the client's money than in working responsibly and appropriately to solve their problem. Be sincere and apply "eye to eye" in your conversations with the customer. If you have nothing to hide, you have nothing to fear, right?

2. Sound the customer's needs well

Try to understand the customer's needs, what he needs or desires, and what will give him satisfaction. This is one of the most important closing techniques for real estate sales and prevents you from offering a property that the client does not need. Thus, it helps you to select the one that exactly meets your needs. Of course, these needs vary according to each person, hence the need for a personalized survey.

A customer may want a three-bedroom apartment in a secure condominium; another may want a small house on the street near the center. The good broker must be prepared to satisfy both.

3. Don't be pushy and inconvenient

The broker can be a little confused when it comes to "persisting" and, at the same time, "not being insistent." There is a limit to insist. Even when the professional is unable to make the sale with a customer on a certain day, he can try on another occasion or with another customer. The annoying broker, the one who seems to be forcing the customer to make a purchase, ends up being avoided and is hardly able to make good sales.

4. Feed your patience

Pay attention to one more of our tips for being a good realtor: you have to be patient! After all, he is trading high-value goods, and people will not simply buy without evaluating, researching, and comparing prices.

5. Get organized and be foresighted

One of the most unpleasant things for the customer when buying real estate is the bureaucracy related to documentation. Visits to the registry office, checking the legality of the property and so on. One of the real estate sales techniques is that the broker must prepare everything before closing the deal (copies of the deed and IPTU, copies of CPF and identity of the owner, and other things). Check if everything is in accordance with the law, if the property can even be sold and if there is a need for a third-party subscription. Never act carelessly. Don't be the broker who sells the property, receives your commission, and leaves the "pineapple for the customer to pee.".

6. Read and learn

Even if you don't have a lot of time, take the time to read some books and extract some valuable sales lessons.

Starting to be a real estate investor does not require special studies or significant investments. I would say that the main tips I can give are:

- To start with, you only need free newspapers of real estate ads, a telephone and the desire to see dozens if not hundreds of houses.
- Apply the rule of 100-10-1. What does the 100-10-1 rule mean? It means I see 100 properties-I make offers for 10 of these- I buy.
- Allies with the real estate agent, I insist particularly more generally on the creation of your team
- Start with small apartments close to where you live
- Always apply a win-win strategy in negotiation
- Never invest your money
- Never be too greedy: it is better to have 90 today, than 100 tomorrow, because tomorrow there is no certainty

Chapter 10: Build Your Real Estate Empire

Making money can be the answer to many people, and they are not wrong, after all, you need to buy food, pay bills, have fun, etc. But that's not all that matters. Work is not just a way to make money. Having a profession can bring many other experiences and new friends. Work should bring personal satisfaction and be pleasurable. Not everyone can do that. To tell the truth, most people work by looking at their watch and hoping it will be time to go. It is worth trying to seek a professional placement in which pleasure is also part of daily work, as it is proven that those who work with what they like to live better. The first step in taking pleasure in work is to try to work with what you like, but for that, you need to find out what your vocation is, what your interests are.

Often, in theory, we can have an idea of the profession, but when we are working, in practice, and difficulties are present, it may not meet the expectations of those who believe it is an ideal profession. You need to take into account three simple tips:

It is important to seek information about the universe of possibilities of work within a profession, only then is it possible to perceive which possibilities of the profession you identify with. To do this, seek to talk to professionals in your area of interest and also research careers that are attractive on the internet. Often, what separates people from a profession is not their temperament, but the lack of some technical skill. Sometimes we face other barriers to follow the imagined career, such as, for example, the lack of physical conditions, the difficulty of access to technical or higher courses, financial restrictions, lack of opportunities, and offers of course or work in the place where we live.

It is often necessary to develop the technical skills that are lacking. Always try to update yourself in the area of information technology, develop a good diction and oratory, know the current legislation, for the area of Real Estate transactions. In addition, make a personal investment: purchase a computer notebook, cell phone, and appropriate clothing. With that, myths and prejudices related to the job market and the career that I would like to follow will be overthrown. This personal investment concerns several things, but the most important of them is to never stop studying and updating yourself.

Imagine you are working in a city where there is a location with an area where there is a great opportunity for growth in the area of real estate transactions, such as a large plot of land that can become a real estate development, for example. The good professional, knowledgeable about the city and the neighborhood, can suggest to the selling client and the buying client a partnership for individualization in lots and for the construction of houses and buildings. See the winning opportunity for this broker, in addition to intermediating the purchase and sale, can assist in the dismemberment of the lots, in the preparation of the documentation and, also, in the dispatch at the bank.

The technician in real estate transactions is a professional trained to inform interested parties about the conditions and advantages of the real estate market, promoting the agreement of their wishes, preparing them to enter into such a contract. The performance of the real estate agent is of great importance to society, as we can consider him as responsible for the formation and development of neighborhoods and cities.

The realtor acts as a mediator between the parties. For those who intend to sell a property, the real estate broker knows what the best days to advertise a property in a certain neighborhood, in which newspaper, in which social networks, so that the best return is achieved, in addition to having the experience to do writing the ad to cover what is necessary in order to attract the attention of potential buyers are. For the exercise of the activity of a real estate broker, preliminary proof of the legal qualification of the professional to exercise the profession is required. This confirmation occurs with the presentation by the interested professional, of the diploma of completion of the technical course, or at a higher level of a specific course in real estate transactions. The courses that enable the professional to act as a realtor are:

- Technical course in real estate transactions
- Degree in real estate business management

The development and growth of businesses in the real estate market have led to the unfolding of tasks carried out by realtors, giving rise to opportunities for the development of other professional activities that go beyond the traditional task of intermediating the purchase and sale or rental of commercial and residential properties. An example that we can bring refers to the performance of the realtor as a document broker who is the agent specialized in researching, searching and obtaining all documents, certificates and declarations of the people involved in the business for the preparation of contracts, purchase commitments and sale, lease, exchange, lease, as well as in the search and obtaining of such documents, aiming at the elaboration of public deeds and the due registration in the notary of the real estate district.

This higher level of knowledge demand for the proper and correct proof of the conditions for doing business has created these other opportunities for professional performance, including in the form of service providers. Another example of diversified professional practice for the real estate broker is as a property appraiser. Who better to evaluate real estate than the one who lives in the real estate market? Of course, property valuation is intended to price with reference to the comparison of property values in the region. Real estate appraisers can act in areas such as real estate appraisers and experts, who prepare the Technical Opinion of Market Valuations (PTAM) to determine the updated value of the real estate for banks, which will be used to:

- The guarantee of financial loan operations
- The judicial or extrajudicial liquidation of overdue loan contracts
- Obtaining the updated value of companies' real estate assets

The exchange of real estate, for example, two apartments, is a practice that is not very widespread yet has some really advantageous aspects. Probably the main difficulty lies in finding two subjects who have a goal that makes them indispensable to each other. But how does the house swap work? There must be a series of combinations in which it is not always easy to run. The seller must first want to sell his real estate unit; then, he must find a buyer, who, in turn, holds a property right on a property, and who is interested in his home. The satisfaction of the respective goods must be reciprocal, and the value of the two units must not differ much. Otherwise, the adjustment due to filling the gap could complicate the negotiation.

What are the advantages of home exchange?

Given the certainty of the combination, the critical issues are minimal, and the advantages rather interesting. This type of procedure allows both parties, who acquire the asset, to take possession of it without taking out a mortgage, as is the case in most cases. Is there a regulation governing this type of sale? Absolutely yes. Obviously, the rules valid for ordinary sales apply, even if in the case of the exchange of properties, at least in the pure one, it does not a passage of money is expected.

What are the types of home exchange?

As mentioned, the exchange can take place if the exchange takes place between units that have more or less the same value. In fact, when there is no adjustment, the exchange is pure. But there may also be the case in which the value of the two goods differs.

Suppose that a person whose apartment is located in Canada decides to sell it at a price of 400,000$. Due to a business transfer to another state, in addition to selling his property, he will also have to find an apartment in his new city. By chance, he may come across a person who has two apartments in his new location and who has the desire to sell one, maybe a studio apartment in the center, perfect for a single. The goal is to make an investment and buy a house in the most beautiful city in the world; for example, he could be willing to make an income from it, transforming his property into a holiday home.

Let's also assume that the value of the two houses differs because of the change in location. It would be a truly first-rate holiday home. The studio apartment in his new location instead costs 300,000$. In this case, the exchange would be possible only for a cash consideration, useful to bridge the value gap between the two assets. More generally, the exchange of properties can be of three types, depending on the owners of the respective properties:

The exchange can, in fact, take place between two private entities. In this case, the exchange is said to be direct; The exchange could be carried out successfully between a private individual and a company, for example, a construction company. In this case, we speak of exchange in consignment. A person decides to buy a new building and to sell an older apartment to the construction company in exchange. It may suit both parties, as the private individual would find himself with a new apartment, perhaps perfectly in accordance with the law and without any need for renovation. On the other hand, however, there is a risk that although the person has already alienated the old one, he may find himself temporarily homeless, because the new construction may not yet be complete. On the other hand, the builder has another need, that of selling all the real estate units under construction. Many of the new apartments remain unsold due to the real estate crisis. The risk for the manufacturer, in this case, is not being able to sell the older apartment and to remain without liquidity. But if both parties agree, the exchange between the two units does not present any difficulties whatsoever. Despite some possible problems in this type of exchange, the exchange between individuals and businesses is always highly quoted.

What are the requirements of the home exchange?

In order for the exchange to go smoothly, it is necessary that the two goods exchanged are free from mortgages and mortgages. The case in which there is a mortgage on one of the two properties is a little less complicated. Certainly, the practices to solve the problem will lengthen the procedures useful for making the exchange, because the property will have to be freed from the constraint of the installments still missing and which are due to the bank that paid the sum. The mortgage could also be turned on both properties being exchanged. What happens in this situation?

1. The new owner can take on the mortgage on the house (for example the first home loan) as soon as the swap and pay off the installments according to the old tariff plan, or he can lean towards the disbursement of a new mortgage that will take the place of what was already there. In this case, the costs of this new payment will be paid.

What are the costs of the exchange? It is one of the additional advantages of the exchange. The costs are certainly lower than a normal purchase. The act by which the exchange is sanctioned is unique; it is a notarial deed whose costs can be divided between the two parties. There are taxes on this type of transaction. However, as in the case of the expenses of the notarial deed, taxes, by law, are also divided between the parties. The Civil Code, in fact, allows the parties involved in the exchange to stipulate and proceed with the registration of a single document that establishes the exchange.

The taxes due to the State are calculated on a single transaction, yet the entity depends on the contracting parties; in fact, the taxes are not always the same. For example, mortgage taxes and those due from the land register are paid only once and have a total amount. Another advantage of the exchange between private individuals is the exemption from stamp duty.

People often have the misconception that if you own a red house for two families, you can exchange it for the same exact red house for two families. This is not true. The main thing is that both old and new properties should be acquired for investment purposes.

The exchange of real estate remains one of the most advantageous ways to sell an apartment and buy a new one. In fact, when an exchange is not made, the most frequent problem is that of not knowing where to stay while waiting for both operations to be successful. In addition, real estate appraisers can be appraisers in legal proceedings, by means of a specific judicial designation for obtaining property values or indemnities, related to the demands for termination of real estate contracts, renegotiation of debts in real estate financing contracts, aiming at the resolution of lawsuits for sharing wills, separation of couples and also for the payment or compensation of expropriations. For any profession, it takes a lot of dedication. In the real estate profession, there are many alternatives to be able to practice the profession.

Chapter 11: How Various Financing Strategies Affect Investment

1) TYPES OF GAIN

The gain in making a real estate investment essentially derives from one or more of the following three mechanisms: (1) the revaluation of a property over time: in particular, if I buy at a minimum of the real estate cycle and sell at a maximum, I can have the greatest profit, however, if I buy to the maximum and resell after only a few years, I risk taking a heavy loss; (1) the capital gain, that is, the difference between the sale and purchase price, which can be made positive, in addition to the strategy just described, also by buying a rented house at a high discount and reselling it free, or by buying a house at a judicial auction at a price lower than the market price and then reselling it, or again, buying the "bare ownership" of property and reselling it when the usufructuary dies; (3) the rent, which represents a monthly income. Of course, in all three cases, the taxes reduce the net profit a little, but they do not change the substance of the speech.

2) HOW TO MAXIMIZE REVALUATION

To derive the maximum profit from the revaluation of a property over time, it is essential (1) to know the real estate cycles and (2) to buy and sell at the right time, because in this type of investment the "timing" is a decisive factor, since from one year to the next in the real estate market there may be variations in the prices that are sometimes "notable," wherewith this adjective we mean a 20% even at 100%. The simplest strategy is to buy a real estate cycle at a minimum and sell at a maximum, although obviously, it is not easy to recognize them if not following the market a little. As we have seen on the page on real estate cycles, however, it is not enough to buy at the minimum of a cycle to make an excellent deal: it is necessary to focus on the properties that tend to reevaluate more over time, namely the prestigious ones located in the center of the large cities. Furthermore, it must be taken into account that the real estate market in large cities starts (or slows down) earlier than in other parts.

3) HOW TO MAXIMIZE INCOME

We can maximize the "capital gain" of a real estate investment - that is, the difference between the sale and purchase price of a property - by adding a second strategy to the strategy of buying at the minimum of a real estate cycle and selling at a maximum. obviously be the only one that can be applied with certain profit when not you are near a minimum of the cycle (that is most of the time): buy a property at auction, where you can even get a discount of 30% on the market price, and then sell it immediately; buy a property already leased, which entails a discount of about 30% on the price compared to a free one, but there is the disadvantage that to sell you have to wait for the tenant to vacate the apartment; buy the "bare ownership" of a house, which entails a percentage discount on the variable price, as it is linked to the age of the usufructuary, but in this case, there is the unknown of the unexpected date of death of the usufructuary to be able to sell.

4) HOW TO MAXIMIZE LEASE INCOME

To maximize the income that can be obtained by renting a property, it is necessary to choose the most "suitable" property. In practice, it is generally better to prefer one or two small apartments - let's say 40-60 square meters - over a large one of 80-120 square meters, because the income that can be obtained by renting them is higher, in proportion to the value of the property. In addition, the apartments that make the most of them, also from the point of view of rents, are those located in large cities, where there is always a great demand. Alternatively, if you are very far from these cities, you can orient yourself to a university city, where you will not have major problems renting them to students if you buy them in the center or, in any case, not far from the university structures. Obviously, to also earn from the difference between the sale price and the purchase price,

5) HOW TO MAXIMIZE THE TOTAL GAIN

The best strategy to maximize total income through a freely chosen real estate investment depends above all on the period of the real estate cycle in which you are located. If you are at a minimum of the cycle, then, in general, it is better to buy a property "at a discount" paying it 20-30% less than the market price (therefore in a judicial auction or already leased) and sell it at the next maximum of the cycle, in the meantime renting it but making sure that you can free it before the maximum of the market. If, on the other hand, you are in an ascending phase of the real estate cycle, it is always advisable to buy the property at a discount to sell it at the maximum of the cycle, but evaluating the feasibility of the thing and - if it was bought at auction - whether to rent it or sell it immediately. Finally, if you are in a phase descending or at a maximum of the real estate cycle, the most sensible option is to "stay still." The purchase of bare ownership, on the other hand, makes sense only if it is done at the minimum of a cycle, but it is an investment that has a very long time horizon.

Chapter 12: Structuring Financial Instruments

Over the past few years, the asset management sector has undergone a profound transformation process that has allowed operators to offer their customers increasingly innovative products and services capable of satisfying the growing demand for new financial products. This is how real estate investment funds are created, which allow you to transform real estate investments, which by their nature, require longer times than investment type investments into shares of financial assets, which allow generating liquidity without the investor having to directly acquire a property. These types of funds, given its ability to preserve value through the passage of time, represents an interesting alternative to traditional investments, especially in those market phases in which the progressive reduction in interest rates makes it attractive invest in real estate. Real estate funds

Real estate funds invest assets of at least two thirds in real estate, real estate rights and investments in real estate companies. They are closed, or they provide a right to reimbursement of the subscribed share only at a certain expiry.

How a real estate fund works

Real estate funds are born with a pre-established initial endowment of assets, variable due to the normal changes in value connected with the appreciation/depreciation of the assets. This patrimony is divided into a predetermined number of shares. The first phase of the birth of a real estate fund starts with its subscription. The fund's objective is, in fact, to collect a certain amount of money from its subscribers (investors), money which will then be used for portfolio management. Subscriptions are open until this amount is reached, subscriptions are closed when the necessary capital is reached. Then there is a second phase, in which, once the money has been collected, the fund selects the properties to be acquired. The properties are selected according to management lines of the fund: some funds favor residential and office buildings, other commercial properties (shopping centers and galleries in particular), still other areas to be built or complexes to be renovated. The units can be subscribed, within the limits of the availability of the fund, only during the offer phase, and the reimbursement normally occurs only at maturity. However, it remains possible to buy or sell them on a regulated market if they are traded there. Listing on a regulated market is required by law and guarantees greater liquidity to the capital. Participants can then repossess the capital invested, plus any capital gains or penalized by the market discount.

Advantages and disadvantages

The main advantage linked to these investment typologies is for the client to get hold of a new investment instrument compared to the traditional ones (mutual funds, bonds, policies, shares) of medium and long term, linked to a type of investment. (real estate) not covered by other instruments or not linked to other indices or markets. The disadvantage, on the other hand, is linked to the fact that the real estate fund is a medium and long-term instrument. Therefore it should, at least in theory, be purchased at the time of issue and kept to maturity. Although many real estate funds are also listed on the stock exchange, and therefore it is possible to negotiate them even before their expiration; instruments remain much less liquid than equities, and it can be more difficult to find a counterpart in the short term.

Unlike normal investment funds, in which an investor can freely subscribe or redeem units, increasing or decreasing the fund's investable funds, a "closed-end fund" determines its size from the start, and once all the money is collected, it is no longer available to other investors.

Obviously, the purchase price may be different from the "NAV" (i.e., the declared value of the real estate portfolio). Buying a real estate fund at a price lower than its "NAV" however does not necessarily mean making a good deal, given that the value of a real estate portfolio cannot be certain. There are, in fact, numerous cases of real estate funds that chronically quote well below the "NAV" declared by the manager.

Real estate funds have an expiration date

Each real estate fund has an expiration date specified on the prospectus; this means that by that date, the real estate portfolio must have been liquidated, and the money returned to investors. This means that the owners of units in the Fund suffer the risk of price fluctuations in the final stage of its life.

This risk can be anything but insignificant, as the investors of the "Portfolio Immobiliare Crescita" Fund, which expired in the second half of 2008, well know, thus suffering the negative consequences of the explosion of the crisis in the sales phase. In some cases, the managers of the Fund may request an extension or "grace period."

REAL ESTATE FUNDS HAVE LEVERAGE

The majority of real estate funds also operate through leverage, borrowing to invest a greater amount than that conferred by subscribers. Obviously, leverage allows greater gains in the event of a rise in property values and vice versa. Furthermore, the possibility of leverage can aggravate the problems of disposal near the expiry date to provide independent analyzes and comments on the financial markets, through periodic reports and real-time interpretations of the main economic events;

Report correct investment strategies through "Recommended Portfolios" updated in real-time. By correct investment strategies we mean a set of choices that allow adequate distribution of risks and give the possibility of obtaining returns above the market average; Contribute to a greater awareness of investors on the most frequent opportunities, risks, errors and misinformation cases in the world of savings;

REAL ESTATE PARTNERSHIP

There are several types of partnerships that can be entered into the real estate sector, such as, for example, autonomous brokers who come together to work in a team with an internal referral system. Real estate agents, in turn, have a fixed staff of brokers, but, in times of high demand, they can enter into temporary partnerships with independent brokers. Finally, there are construction companies that are always looking for partnerships, especially when large projects are about to be launched.

Partnerships are, in general, advantageous or at least necessary for both sides. Suppose a situation in which you have a customer looking for a property with specific characteristics that you do not currently have in your portfolio. You can then contact a partner broker who owns the property and check its availability.

The next steps will depend on the agreement between you, and it may be that you pass on the client to continue with the negotiation, or it may be that your partner allows you to negotiate his property with the client. Naturally, the profits will be divided according to the participation of each one in the business, or partnership contracts previously signed will determine the amounts to be received. The great advantage in these cases is that you were able to fulfill a customer's desire, generating profit today, and possible recommendations in the future.

The situation mentioned above illustrates a possible partnership between two brokers or even brokers and real estate agents, but in this post, we will see how brokers can enter into partnerships with builders or developers. We will discuss how such partnerships should be made and also what the advantages of this union are.

Why partner with construction companies?

Large builders and developers carry out frequent launches of buildings and housing estates with a wide range of properties that, as they are new and modern, present several advantages for those who buy them. It can be said, therefore, that these companies move businesses with high General Sales Value.

On the other hand, the commissions offered by construction companies are lower than those offered by real estate agents. Thus, the great advantage of closing partnerships with construction companies is the large volume of sales and deals that can be closed each month, due to the high demand and acceptance of their properties. This justifies the fact that several brokers who work together with construction companies have monthly earnings much higher than the average.

Another advantage is the reduction in marketing expenses since the construction companies are already investing heavily in publicizing their projects, with advertisements that are placed on the radio in the region, television, and mainly on the internet. Additionally, pamphlets and banners are placed in high circulation points in the city. Not to mention the fact that some construction companies even invest in the decoration of buildings to serve as a demonstration. All this investment greatly facilitates the work of the construction partners' brokers. A final advantage is a fact that several construction companies offer conditions similar to real estate, covering the costs of their brokers.

How to partner with construction companies

It is possible to realize that for the broker, this scenario is very advantageous,

-Be professional and special in your presentation

With so many advantages, there is no point in thinking that you will be the only broker interested in partnering with construction companies. To get ahead, it is important to show that you are a serious and committed professional. Present your main professional achievements, mention big deals made or situations that show your ability to be productive, such as selling a high volume of real estate in a relatively short period of time.

If you already have a property sales platform, introduce it to your possible new partner. Show the various capabilities of the platform that can help boost sales, such as its own website, contract generator, complete real estate CRM, among others.

-Do good Real Estate Networking

It is easier for a professional who has a wide network of contacts to close new partnerships. This is because people who have partnered with you before may be willing to introduce you to new partners. Even if your contacts do not have enough influence to indicate to those responsible for the project, they can inform you of the opportunity, which is especially useful if they have this information with some exclusivity or in advance.

-Analyze the construction company's history

Before closing partnerships with construction companies, it is a good idea to seek information from other projects in the same, check if the delivery date was according to expectations and if the customers were satisfied with the investment.

Although the monetary and legal consequences in these cases do not affect the brokers involved as much, it is always good to work with serious and committed companies. Another point to consider is that a dissatisfied customer is unlikely to come to you for a new business or make positive recommendations about you in the future.

-Officialize the partnership terms in a contract

Never close a deal or partnership with just a handshake. It is important to write contracts that establish the rights and responsibilities of each of the parties involved. This is important for both the construction company and the broker because, in this way, both have a legal document for future consultation, if necessary. Enjoy and make available the properties and related information on your own website. In most cases, the construction company has already done and continues to do a marketing campaign in the region. You can and should still inform your own customers of the new opportunity. Use marketing automation tools like Ville Target to send messages to your email marketing list and to create interesting landing pages that capture your customers' attention and interest.

A good performance, with high sales numbers, does not only mean profits in the present moment but also the possibility of new partnerships in the future.

Chapter 13: Marketing Strategy

There are two basic elements you need to keep in mind when it comes to marketing:

- What your customers want.
- What you can offer your customers.

A good agent must obviously be able to combine the two sides of the coin, and he must do it extremely well. Any small deficiency or weakness in this area will surely make your customers, current and above all potential, run by other agents of your competitors. Since selling and renting properties are the basis of your career, we will focus on sharing unique real estate marketing strategies that allow you to promote and sell your properties effectively and efficiently. Adopting strategic elements that go outside the box could be what you need to get the much sought-after competitive advantage over other agents.

1. Seeing is believing

Don't you find it strange that the biggest purchases we make in our lives are mostly "blind"? Before spending tens of thousands of dollars on a car, you usually have the chance to try it out. We can touch it and feel it with our hands. Why could all this not be possible even for something for which hundreds of thousands of dollars will be spent? Yes, it is true, a great help in this sense is given by the Open House, where the customer enters a house, takes photos and creates a concrete idea of his future. But unfortunately, all this only partially approaches the experience of actually living inside a given apartment. Buying a house is a decision strongly linked to emotions and feelings, so what better way to stimulate the right emotions if not providing a real 360 ° experience of the apartment in order to try out what their life will be like before buying it? This real estate marketing strategy could also prevent any waste of time due to buyers not really interested in a specific property.

Offering this type of opportunity to your customers not only demonstrates your ability to take advantage of new technologies, always keeping you in a cutting-edge position, but also proves that your interests go far beyond the realization of the maximum profit deriving from the sale of a flat. Ultimately, show your willingness to find the perfect person/family for a particular home. This will allow you to increase trust not only in the agent-buyer relationship. But also in the relationship that develops between the agent and the owner.

2. Make them make friends with their surroundings

Often the peculiarities of a neighborhood and the services present in a certain area can help you sell a house better than any other aspect. The main problem, in this case, is that potential buyers do not know the neighborhood well, and therefore they have a lot of difficulty in terms of how their life could be in this new area. Similarly to what has been seen above, leveraging new technologies allows you to offer your potential buyer a unique, real, and profound service and experience. How can we put this into practice? Use apps like Uber to offer your customers an unforgettable experience in what will be their future neighborhood of residence. It's all much simpler than you think. And why, even in this case, should it work? Only very few buyers bother to explore a certain area before buying or renting a new apartment. For this reason, there is no better way to start getting to know a neighborhood, than to go out for a nice dinner without having to worry about figuring out which is the right way to get to the restaurant and without the risk of getting lost continuously. Furthermore, the fact that your customers are not driving the car will also allow them to notice details of the neighborhood that they would otherwise never have seen. This real estate marketing strategy, like the previous one, not only proves your technical skills but also demonstrates your real interest in the customer, looking for both the right home and the right neighborhood.

3. Make them feel part of the community

One of the main emotional barriers that arise when buying a house is precisely the concern and insecurity of not feeling accepted within a new community. An effective way to help potential customers become part of the neighborhood is, for example, organizing a meeting through the MeetUp app in the property for sale, in order to allow current members of the community to share useful tips for improving the neighborhood itself.

Also, in this case, the procedure is very simple: access the application and create your "meetup," invite the people you want taking care to include with your customers also their future neighbors, as well as the most relevant members to the within the community.

Why should it work? Despite the many ways that exist today to meet and create relationships with the rest of the world, it still remains difficult for some people to develop relationships with others, especially if they are catapulted into a completely new and unfamiliar place. The organization of these meetings will ensure that your customers are fully immersed in the neighborhood reality, thus managing to develop a good knowledge of the people who live there and the main dynamics that characterize it. All this will certainly have a fundamental role in the sale of the house: by organizing a "meetup" in the property you are selling you could not only create the right atmosphere to insert your customers within a certain community, but your way of working could also arouse the interest of some neighbors, who may unexpectedly become your customer. So consider this real estate marketing strategy as a real business card!

4. Maximize opportunities

Have you ever spent whole days waiting in vain for customers in your Open House, organized with a lot of effort, but without getting the desired results? I imagine that in many cases, the answer is yes: no matter how good you are from a marketing point of view, but this little inconvenience will have happened to you at least once in your real estate career. All of these real estate marketing strategies can have great benefits on your reputation as an agent. They are creative ideas, which aim to push you beyond your comfort zone when it comes to selling a certain property.

Conclusion

The number of real estate transactions is constantly growing. Part of the premises was purchased so that the buyer could save a large amount of money from inflation and try to make a profit from it. In other words, real estate investment is not as rare as it was a decade ago. Despite the fact that in many areas of investment, the income is not too high, and the risks are significant, the investment process itself is a necessary thing. Another thing is that real estate investments have recently earned a dubious reputation. And there are reasons for this: long cost recovery. The income from renting out real estate for rent is actually not as high as we would like. The moment of payback (taking into account the costs incurred) may never come. Doubtful liquidity. Real estate in our country is easily losing value. In addition, when selling earlier than three years later, an income tax is levied on the amount received, which can nullify all attempts to earn money. High associated costs (utilities, taxes, maintenance of real estate in good condition); rapid obsolescence of real estate. With the speed with which construction is being carried out in our country, new buildings are "aging" rather than their owners. In addition, the acquired apartment in a new building, even after one owner becomes a "secondary." And the secondary housing market is going through hard times. People prefer housing in a new building for many reasons, including because preferential loans are provided for housing in new houses.

There are those who speak of the real estate crisis and those of the recovery market. There are those who say that now it is no longer time to invest money in real estate, and those who, like us, claim that today is really the best time to do it!

The house, however, has always been an indispensable asset and remains so! It is the first thing you think of buying as soon as you have some money aside, undoubtedly, until a few decades ago, the "brick" was, by all accounts, certainly the best investment possible, because it was thought that the value of the properties was always, inevitably, destined to go up. So it was, until at some point, thanks to the economic crisis, property prices plummeted and those who had recently bought a house and then, for some reason, despite themselves, found themselves having to sell it, went against big losses. Clearly, like any other market, the real estate market is also subject to ups and downs (it is quite obvious!), But unlike the financial one, knowing the rules of the game and paying a little attention, it is always possible to generate profits: l business is at hand, both in times of prosperity and in times of crisis, you just need to know how to recognize it!

Investing in real estate is not something for a select few! It is absolutely not necessary to have five or six zero digits, a few tens of thousands of dollars are enough to obtain a comfortable monthly income that allows you to be able to take away some more whim! Paradoxically, the best way to invest is to do it without money, so much so that, as we have already seen in a previous article, it is possible to obtain an excellent income even from non-owned properties! You don't have to think that investing in real estate means buying an extra luxury villa or a penthouse in the center: these are not the real estate deals! It is unfair to have the preconception that the real estate sector is a corrupt sector, full of unscrupulous people, driven only by the intention of making money! It is not so! Even among real estate developers, there are more or less serious ones, but many, just like me, do this job with the heart and with passion, with the hope of improving the reality and the city in which they live and happy to give each the home of their dreams. Those who do real estate with love do not do it by disfiguring the landscape to the detriment of others and future generations, only in the name of profit, so much so that in many years of honored career I have built very little, but rather I have oriented myself towards the recovery and enhancement of the existing building stock. Obviously, as in any other business, you cannot make all the grass a bundle, and you cannot improvise real estate investors overnight. It is essential to know the area in which you operate and the dynamics that animate it, but everyone can learn. Good real estate deals are always there! The important thing is to know how to find and recognize them. Never before has hurry be a bad adviser. You have to be patient and not get carried away by easy enthusiasm. It is certainly always advisable to start gradually and without overdoing it, especially if you go into this sector independently and are not experts in the field.

There are many and different ways to invest in real estate, depending on how much you are willing to get involved, but, for example, if you classically decide to buy a property to make it income renting it you will not have to look for it as if it became your home, you will have to think in a different perspective. The parameters to be taken into account are innumerable, starting from the palatability of the area and the type of average catchment area it has, but remember: you won't have to live there! You don't have to think about your needs and your tastes!

You must fall in love with the deal and not with the house you are about to buy! Normally it is better to buy a house "in bad shape," but with great potential than a new one or almost: you can win it at a good price and rearrange it properly. In fact, this is what we do: we buy properties, mostly made up of different apartments, and we refurbish them, creating a profit margin!

Remember: real estate business is done when you buy a property, almost never when you sell! You have to find not only the right house but also the right seller. The reasons why it sells are innumerable: transfers, separations, children who are born, children who grow up, families who have to shrink or expand. Everyone has their own reasons for selling: to make a good deal, and you need to identify the most motivated sellers, those who actually need and hurry to conclude the deal, instead of avoiding those who can afford to wait and want to achieve the required amount. Good deals are always there, so another advice is: don't get too tired! Keep in mind your goal, and if the deal you had sniffed does not go through patience! Tomorrow you will probably be able to buy another property, perhaps even more profitable. In spite of what you may think, it is not the most expensive and prestigious properties that guarantee the greatest profits. Even for those with significant capital available in principle, it is better to invest in 10 two-room apartments of 100,000 dollars each to be rented than in an extra-luxury one-million penthouse!

There are countless and all different possibilities to invest in the real estate market, to do so it is not necessary to buy an entire property in full autonomy, also because not everyone can afford it and many then would not know how to manage it, either in terms of renovation or leasing.

Lightning Source UK Ltd.
Milton Keynes UK
UKHW050632260821
389509UK00005B/180